'Now tell me - how about you?'

Poetry to share with older people

Gill Johnson and Marilyn McGregor

'Now tell me - how about you?'

Poetry to share with older people

Marilyn and Gill have worked in many care and nursing homes designing and delivering activities for residents, including those living with dementia. Gill's original poetry is an important part of their work as it encourages reminiscence. Their company, Bonnie Day, is an organisation that is highly acclaimed for work with older people, carers and families.

www.bonnie-day.co.uk

Foreword

'Now tell me - how about you. ~~is a collection of~~ original poems based on life in post-war Britain. They are written to support people who visit older friends, relatives or clients and sometimes need interesting topics to engage them. Set in the 1940s, 1950s and 1960s, the poems also prompt reminiscence which can make you laugh, smile and sometimes even shed a tear together.

'Now tell me - how about you?' are poems that have been enjoyed by older people, including those living with dementia, in care or in their own homes. We would like to share with you this collection of original poetry. We have first hand experience of enjoying these poems with older people. We know how stimulating and comforting they can be, wherever they are read.

'You have brought my husband back to me...' A relative, after a poetry reading.

5

'Now tell me - how about you?' provides notes to help you talk about the poems with your relative. We call them 'Reminiscence Avenues' as they are ways to prompt memories. These 'Reminiscence Avenues' are presented in different forms, including questions, prompts, quizzes and useful vocabulary. We also suggest things that you can do together during your visit and in the future.

Very positive feedback from carers and families has encouraged us to make our poems available to a wider audience.

Enjoy reading these poems together.

Contents

'Now tell me - how about you?'

Poetry to share with older people

Top Tips for sharing these poems with your older relatives and friends

NB: We are using the term 'relative' throughout to mean relative, friend, client or patient.

- Choose the poems to read out with your relative in mind
- If the poem is seasonal it may mean more to read it in the appropriate season
- Try to have a setting free from distractions
- Give yourselves time to read the poems and do the activities
- When reading the poems try not to rush; it is more important to read with expression
- Make a few gentle gestures or actions to bring the poem alive as you read
- If you have any objects relevant to the poem these could be useful to help evoke memories

- Speak quietly at the end of the rhyming line and your relative may join in
- As you read the poem be aware of what verses your relative liked best so you can talk about them afterwards
- Read the poem again if your relative really liked it

Enjoy!

Playing out

I remember all those games I played
In endless summer childhood days:
Jacks, marbles, skittles, hula-hoops,
Dolls, prams, cat's cradles, string in loops.

Chalking grids with a stone in the street,
We'd hopscotch, hop, hop, hopping on our feet.
Chanting clapping songs, my friend and me
About 'A sailor who went to sea, sea, sea.'

Skipping with ropes both short and long
Singing together our rhythmic song.
'Jelly on a plate, Sausage in a pan,
A house to let, Beware the Bogie man.'

In school we had balls to throw and catch,
A chase at play with kisses to snatch!
At home, old blankets made a safe house,
Underneath, tea with Ted Bear and Mouse.

There was a rope swing by the river
Jumping across made us shiver,
We'd run, catch, tightly cling and fly,
Whooping, screaming, lifting our feet high.

What fun we had in years gone by
As time passes on, I think with a sigh,
Yes, I remember those games I played
In endless summer childhood days.

I too, remember all those games I played,
In endless summer childhood days:
Playing 'war' with battered tin hats,
Sliding on tummies like hunting cats.

Cowboys and Indians, twig bow in hand,
Planning manoeuvres, writing in sand.
Stretching, scratching, high into trees,
Splintered branches, dirty hands and knees.

Wonky pirate puppets made from socks,
Dinky cars shiny, in a bright new box.
Rip, rip ripping to get the new treasure
Rolling them downstairs; CRASH! What a
pleasure.

Cricket in the summer, a willow bat to swing,
Then scrumping apples, conkers on a string.
Pockets of marbles, flat stones in a pile,
Skimming over water, a 'three' made us smile.

Fishing in the cut, a 'boat' from a log,
The rough and tumble of 'British Bulldog'.
Knocking on doors and running away
Breathless energy in the games we played.

What fun we had in years gone by
As time passes on I, too, think with a sigh,
Yes, I remember those games I played
In endless summer childhood days.

PLAYING OUT

Sharing this poem with your relative:

'Playing out' was a favourite pastime for many children from the 1940's.

Children used to play out on the streets, down the rec, (recreation ground) and wherever there was an open space including bombsites. In those days, children were creative, making up their own games like 'Hide and Seek,' 'It,' 'Catch,' 'Tin Tan Tommy,' or 'British Bulldog' and many skipping rhymes. Boys and girls often played separately and games went in and out of fashion according to the season. Playing out all day was fun especially in the long summer holidays. Meals were seen as an irritating interruption and at bedtime, cries of 'Just five minutes more… please!' were usually heard.

Reminiscence Avenues

After you have read these poems which look at playing out from a girl's and a boy's memories, it

14

is useful to have some prompt questions ready to evoke memories about playing out. Read out our questions below to stimulate conversation.

Questions

What games do you remember playing in your childhood?

What games were your favourites; can you remember any of the rules?

Were there any games you didn't like playing? Why?

Can you remember the names of any friends you played with?

Where did you play your childhood games?

What time did you have to come in; were you told off if you were late?

The poem mentions the 'Bogie man'; can you remember what that means?

What games did you play in your school playground?

What games did you play in the garden, in the park, by the river, or in the woods?

Did you play out on your own, in a small group or a large gang?

Top Tip: Objects relevant to this poem could include: Skipping rope, teddy bears, dolls, football, tennis ball, marbles, hoops and five stones.

Personal Reminiscences:

'I remember rolling marbles in the gutter...'

'All the games stopped when we heard the 'Tonibell' chimes of the ice cream van.'

'We used to make kites from old newspaper and string...'

At the pictures

When I was much younger,
The cinema was a treat,
We used to get dressed up for it
And went looking very neat.

It might have been the Odeon,
The Gaumont or the Ritz
And we always saw two films,
The news and advertising bits.

On Saturday morning
Our children went to see
Froghorn Leghorn and other films
As the 'Minors of the ABC'.

I loved going to the pictures
I loved to see the flicks
I was really mesmerised
By Lassie's clever tricks.

Film stars were very handsome
Whether in colour or black and white
We settled in the 1 and 9s
Anticipating the sight.

Rugged Rock Hudson,
In comedy with Doris Day,
Grace Kelly and Frank Sinatra
In High Society did play.

The wonderful Western films,
Starring the brave John Wayne
And the British Bobby
Jack Warner was his name.

Elegant Audrey Hepburn,
With Cat upon her knee,
Lived a glamorous lifestyle
And had Breakfast at Tiffany.

So many famous faces,
Alistair Sim, James Stewart came,
Brynner, Brando and Bette Davis
So many I could name.

We sang with Judy Garland
Red shoes on a yellow brick road,
We marvelled at Monroe's beauty
And Liz Taylor's eyes really glowed.

Then there was the interval
With usherettes and trays,
We'd buy a tub of ice cream
And eat it straightaway.

With Disney fantasy and great plots
We were transported in our seats,
Around the world from east to west
Yes, the cinema was the best of treats.

AT THE PICTURES

Sharing this poem with your relative:

Years ago, going to the 'pictures' or the 'flicks' was a very popular pastime. People would go two or three times a week to see different films, often queuing to get in. Children went to Saturday morning pictures and many adventures were left on a 'cliff hanger' until the next week. However by the next week, the situation had miraculously resolved itself and the hero was saved for another episode. Two films were always shown, the A film and usually a shorter B film. These were shown continuously and, if you liked, you could sit through the films again. The National Anthem was played at the end of the evening and everyone stood up.

Reminiscence Avenues

The poem mentions some of the most famous film stars. However, the list is endless, here are some more suggestions.

Prompts:

Fred Astaire, Humphrey Bogart, Richard Burton, Clark Gable, Tony Curtis, Charlton Heston, Bob Hope, Trevor Howard, Gene Kelly, John Mills, Mickey Rooney

Bette Davis, Rita Hayworth, Katharine Hepburn, Veronica Lake, Betty Grable, Jane Russell, Ginger Rogers, Jean Simmons, Ingrid Bergman, Lana Turner

Photo Album

Create your own photo album of your relative's favourites. Write out the names of the film stars underneath the picture. Talk about their hairstyles, make up, what films they starred in, who they were married to and the names of their children.

Top Tip: Remember to include black and white pictures of film stars as well as colour as they are very evocative of the 1940's and 1950's.

Personal Reminiscences:

'Every week the man at the ABC Minors asked for all the children whose birthday it was to go and stand on the stage. I went up every week!'

'I went to see 'Snow White' and we took a quarter pound of Milk Tray in a purple box. What a treat!'

'We played 'The Wizard of Oz' in the playground at school. That film was marvellous – it changed from black and white to colour.'

Winter

Do you remember waking up
When snow had fallen in the night?
How quiet it was outside the house
When the world turned wintry white.

Do you remember how light it was
Before pushing the curtains back?
And seeing icy fern pictures
Jack Frost's filigree track.

Do you remember how bitter it was
As you reluctantly got out of bed?
Noses cold in the Arctic air,
Chill lino under your tread.

Do you remember how we got dressed
Ready to brave the raw day?
Vests, jumpers, socks and hats
And black wellingtons ready to play.

Do you remember the excitement we felt
As we rushed out of the front door?
Stepping onto the blanket of snow,
Fresh white, then footprints galore.

Do you remember how we played?
Making snowballs oh so round,
Fat snowmen with old pipes
And coal for eyes we found.

Do you remember how our hands froze?
Our gloves just dangled on strings.
Cheeks glowing, noses running
But we didn't notice these things.

Do you remember the fun we had?
Making slides across the path,
Sledges made from old tin trays
How it made us laugh.

Do you remember how the road looked?
The houses swathed in snow,
Trees with a sugary frosting,
Lights in windows all a-glow.

Do you remember the gardens?
Not a chirrup from a bird,
Icicles dangling from gutters
Boundaries snow covered and blurred.

Do you remember going to school?
Our fingers hurting, we cried.
The milk was put by the heater
As it was frozen from lying outside.

Do you remember coming home
On a darkening winter's eve?
Shivering, then warmed by the fire
And a Bovril we may receive.

But do you remember the cold?
And how it made parents ill,
And those awful chilblains
When we toasted feet that were chill.

Do you remember the hard winters?
1947 and '63, I suppose
When it was so very cold
Parts of the River Thames froze.

How do you remember winter?
Cold and damp and grey
Or soft with falling snowflakes?
Making a splendid winter's day.

WINTER

Sharing this poem with your relative:

Winters seemed very cold in post-war Britain. The majority of homes did not have central heating and many people woke up to ice which had formed on the inside of their windows. There was a reliance on coal, coke and paraffin to heat homes. The smell of paraffin in your home is something that you never forget.

In big cities journeys often had to be made in yellow smogs or 'pea-soupers'. It was difficult to see your hand in front of your face.

Two winters that were particularly harsh and memorable were 1947 and 1962/3.

Reminiscence Avenues

After you have read the poem once or twice, reminisce with your relative about winter and what it meant to them.

Watch your relative as you read to see if any particular lines are stimulating memories.

It can be useful to have some vocabulary prepared ready to use.

The words and phrases will mean different things to different people.

Here are just a few to get you started in our Pick 'N' Mix selection.

Pick 'N' Mix

Winter, snowman, snow, frost, scarves

Woollies, icicles, snowballs, ice, boots

Skidding, sliding, skating, trekking, playing

Sledging, throwing, falling, skiing, building

Stunning, ghostly, gleaming, glistening, frosty

Beautiful, dangerous, exciting, breathtaking, adventurous

Top Tip: If you read this poem on a wintry day it will have more impact.

Personal Reminiscences:

'We used to make a sledge from a dustbin lid…'

'We used to have competitions to make the biggest snowball – after the snow had gone, they still remained for a while.'

'We had to clear the paths with shovels – but I'd rather be out with my friends making slides…'

Hats, hats, hats

I've had a lot of hats, since the day I was born,
Yes there's lots of hats that in my life I've worn.

My tiny baby's woolly hat, which I wore in a
pram,
A straw Easter bonnet – which on my head I'd
cram.

At school I had a beret, navy blue with a badge
And when my friend forgot her's – mine she tried
to cadge.

When it rained, I wore a rain hat, in the sun, one
with a brim
Then a very tight rubber one each time I went to
swim.

My Dad had a panama, my Grandpa wore a cap,
My brother a cowboy one, with a dangling strap.

On special occasions, my Mum always looked so
fine
Trimmed in silk and flowers, her face just
seemed to shine.

I remember our next-door neighbour, Auntie Jo
Never wore a hat – but a scarf tied with a bow.

In hospital the nurses had hats to cover their hair
When looking after patients with great respect
and care.

Firemen had hard hats, and some policeman too,
Guardsmen wore a busby, sailors' hats were
white and blue.

Getting married, on my head I wore a veil of lace
Whilst walking down the aisle hopefully with
grace.

So… woolly hats for new-borns, I then knitted with great care,
And wondered what sorts of hats in their life they'd wear…

HATS, HATS, HATS

Sharing this poem with your relative:

Hats were very popular in the 1940s, 1950s and early 1960s worn frequently by men and women alike. People would comment that they did not feel dressed if they were not wearing a hat. For ladies the pillbox was the day wear hat of the 1950s and its evening wear counterpart was the cocktail hat. Men wore bowler hats to the office and men from the working classes wore cloth caps. School children wore berets, boaters and caps.

Another name for a hat, usually a lady's hat, was called a 'titfa' which was Cockney rhyming slang for a hat - 'tit for tat'.

Fashions were often dictated by film stars, famous people and later pop stars, for example the 'Donovan Cap' of the 1960s.

Reminiscence Avenues

This poem really comes alive when you have a

small collection of hats in front of you. Just find hats that you have in the house to begin with. Do not forget to include headscarves as women in the 1940s and 50s frequently wore these. If hats are not available, then some photos or clippings from magazines might be helpful. The questions below will help to evoke memories of all the many occasions when people wore hats.

Questions

What hats can you remember wearing?

What hats did you have to wear to school?

What hats did you wear for playing sports?

What jobs did you have to wear a hat for?

What special occasions did you wear a hat for?

Did you have a favourite hat?

What hat did Tommy Cooper / Charlie Chaplin / John Wayne / Bing Crosby / Sherlock Holmes / Jackie Kennedy wear? (Fez, Bowler, Stetson, Trilby, Deerstalker, Pillbox)

What was Ena Sharples in 'Coronation Street' famous for wearing? (A hair net)

Who wore a hat with 10/6d on it in 'Alice in Wonderland'? (Mad Hatter)

Can you finish the proverb: 'If the cap fits… ?' ('wear it.') What does this mean?

Top Tip: Have a hand mirror ready so relatives can see themselves; this often brings lots of smiles.

Personal Reminiscences:

'I loved knitting bonnets for babies – I knitted all my children's hats.'

'On the way home from school, my friend posted my beret and I had to wait for the postman to get it out for me. I didn't dare go home without it.'

'We used to make paper hats for parties. At school we always made paper hats for the Christmas party.'

A night out

We liked to go out on a night
A change from the wireless voice
Some outside fun, laughs a ton
We had a little choice…

On Monday to the cinema show
We could view a film or two,
Some dashing stars, in fantastic cars
Even though you had to queue.

On Tuesday it could be the Bingo
With pencils poised on pads,
'Clickety click, it's sixty six'
Losing is not so bad...

On Wednesday it maybe cards night
Down at the Railwayman's pub.
Playing whist is our tryst
Diamonds, spades, hearts, clubs.

On Thursday we could be active
Swimming in the pool,
Splashing feet, quite a treat
Then a cuppa, to help us refuel.

On Friday, perhaps, the theatre
A play upon a stage,
Pounding boards, clashing swords
Entertainment for any age.

On Saturday we could dine out
At 'The Restful Tray',
Minute steak, an apple bake
A romantic hideaway.

And Saturdays were the best
More things were on to do,
There was a chance, to go and dance,
A quickstep, two by two.

On Sunday we could go for a walk
To the 'Old Chain Ferry'
A pint of beer, in good cheer
Or for me, a glass of sherry.

So every night we could go out
And do a lot of things, if able,
If money allowed, join a crowd
But mainly…
      we loved tea at our own table.

A NIGHT OUT

Sharing this poem with your relative:

Years ago, people were not glued to their television screens although the wireless was very popular. Most people could not afford to go out every evening. However going to the cinema, the pub or a whist drive was an enjoyable thing to do. In the 1960s if people went for a meal, they often enjoyed a T-bone steak accompanied by a glass of Liebfraumilch.

Reminiscence Avenues

After you have read the poem once, perhaps read it again, but stop after every verse and talk about the contents of that verse. It is likely that your relative enjoyed certain outings more than others. When discussing this poem with your relative concentrate on the outings you know that they liked. Remember too, they may surprise you by mentioning something that you did not know about.

We have included some questions that may evoke memories.

Verse by Verse

What was your favourite night out?

Who was your favourite film star?

When you played Bingo the caller would have phrases to go with certain numbers. Say the first part of the phrases below and see if your relative can remember the phrase or number that came next: Kelly's eye – number 1

Doctor's orders – number 9

Legs eleven - wolf whistle – number 11

Key of the door - 21

Two little ducks - quack quack 22

Two fat ladies – 88

What card games did you play?

What sports did you play?

What plays / pantomimes / musicals did you see at the theatre?

Did you have a favourite restaurant; tell me about it please?

Did you like to go out for a walk? Where did you go?

Top Tip: If your relative liked playing Bingo in the past arrange to play a game with the whole family.

Personal Reminiscences:
'We didn't have much money but often we went for a walk around the houses.'

'I used to go to the Whist Drive at the local swimming pool…'

'Dancing… dancing was always a favourite. I went out almost every Saturday to the Palais before I was married.'

My garden

Walking round my garden –
There's nowhere I'd rather be,
Out in the fine, fresh air
With lots of things to see.

The tallness of the lofty trees,
The wind through white-limbed birch,
Fragrant walnut, apple and pear
With branches for birds to perch.

Soft scented flowers facing the sun,
Grown with tender care;
Carpets of scent and colour
To cut and then to share.

I love to be in the garden,
With spade and fork in hand,
To turn the rich brown soil
And make my mark upon the land.

I like to sit in the garden.
Listen to bees busy in the bed,
The spray of water in the fountain
A hedgehog by the shed.

You can find me in my garden
In wellingtons bright green,
Pushing my trusty wheelbarrow
Or my lawn mowing machine.

There's nowhere like a garden
For peace, calm and pleasure,
Whether it is your own or in a park,
There's always moments to treasure.

MY GARDEN

Sharing this poem with your relative:

People often have lovely memories of their gardens, patios, window boxes and allotments. Like today, many people enjoyed gardening in post-war Britain. Colourful roses, dahlias and chrysanthemums were popular flowers to grow. People often cultivated vegetables for the table and some kept chickens and rabbits for the pot. Percy Thrower has been described as Britain's first celebrity gardener. He hosted BBC's 'Gardening Club' from 1956.

Reminiscence Avenues

Most people have favourite flowers, plants, trees, vegetables and herbs that they can remember. If they are not able to recall names they might recognise the smell of a summer rose, a sprig of lavender or a bunch of parsley.

Prompts:

Before you read this poem maybe have a small table or tray of pictures of flowers, plants, trees, vegetables and herbs from the Internet or magazines. Choose those that you know your relative really likes, may have grown in the past or even won prizes for in shows.

Find pictures that represent the different seasons too:

Spring - Daffodils, tulips, bluebells, primroses, apple blossom

Summer - Roses, pinks, fuchsias, lavender, honeysuckle

Autumn - Chrysanthemums, dahlias, Autumn crocus, conkers, acorns, walnut leaves, plums

Winter - Hellebores, snowdrops, winter flowering jasmine, holly, conifer (pine)

Photo Album

Make your own photo album with pictures of gardens, flowers, vegetables and trees that can be looked at and discussed again and again.

Top Tip: Taking a trip around the garden to smell the flowers is a wonderful thing to do. If that is not possible, pay a visit to a garden centre or watch a gardening programme on the television.

Personal Reminiscences:
'I loved growing vegetables, cabbages, carrots and beans.'

'I won prizes at the local show for my onions and asters.'

'I loved having a garden – but wouldn't want to mow the lawn every week now!'

Beside the sea

What can we see beside the sea?
Golden sands that stretch for yards,
Patrolled with care by safety lifeguards,
Tall, craggy cliffs and long promenades,
Shops with rubber rings and gaudy postcards.

What can we do beside the sea?
Swimming and jumping over a wave,
Building castles with bucket and spade,
Rock pool searching, exploring a cave,
Climbing cliffs and being brave.

What can we hear beside the sea?
The screech and wheel of hungry gulls,
The throb of motorboat as it pulls,
Swish of the sea forming channels
Cry of a seller, 'Fresh shrimps and cockles'.

What can we smell beside the sea?

Hot battered fish, vinegary chips,

Diesel oil whilst on 'Round-the-Bay trips'.

The salt of the water as the wind whips,

Sun cream pouring as the bottle tips.

What can we eat beside the sea?

Candy floss, ice cream, lollies to hold

Hot dog sausages and fizzy drinks cold,

Huge battered fish, a sight to behold,

Sweet sticks of rock in pink, blue and gold.

What is it like beside the sea?

Sitting on a stripy deckchair

Breathing in the salty air,

Sunglasses on against the glare,

Relaxing and enjoying – I wish I was there!

BESIDE THE SEA

Sharing this poem with your relative:

In the 1940s, 50s and 60s it was commonplace that people went on holiday to the seaside in the UK for a week or sometimes two. There was often a 'Factory Fortnight' or 'Wakes Week' when lots of workers had a holiday at the same time. People stayed in caravans, bed and breakfasts or small hotels. At that time, holiday camps were growing in popularity such as Butlin's or Pontin's.

Reminiscence Avenues

After you have read the poem once or twice, reminisce with your relative about going to the seaside and what it meant to them. Watch your relative as you read the poem to see if any particular lines are stimulating memories. It can be useful to have some vocabulary prepared ready to use. The words and phrases below will mean different things to different people.

Pick 'N' Mix

Piers, sand, buckets, spades, deckchairs

Shows, sandcastles, seagulls, fish and chips, sticks of rock

Swimming, jumping, building, exploring, climbing

Relaxing, bathing, paddling, laughing, promenading

Sunny, rainy, colourful, hot, shivery

Funny, exciting, memorable, relaxing, magical

Photo album

Look at some old holiday photos with your relative.

Top Tip: A small collection of postcards, shells and stones can often evoke memories of holidays.

Personal Reminiscences:

'I remember the donkey rides on the sand at Blackpool...'

'The stones on the beach at Hastings really hurt my feet.'

'Mum would pack us some sandwiches and we got on the bus and had a day at the seaside…'

Washday blues

Monday was washday, without a doubt
It was time to get the washtub out.

Monday mornings bright and early
The kitchen, a laundry became,
With a tub of boiling hot water,
Starting the cleaning game.

We opened a packet of Persil,
Daz, Omo, Fairy Snow or Tide,
Sprinkled onto the clothes in the water
For delicates, Lux Flakes were tried.

The clothes were sorted by colour,
Pushed by wooden tongs and swished
Churning about in the washtub
Buffeted, just as my Mum wished.

You could smell the washing water,
You could hear the hiss of steam,
The clothes whirled round in a bundle,
Mum pounded to get them clean.

The collars and cuffs that were dirty
Before they were sunk in the wash
Were scrubbed with green Fairy soap
And given an extra hard slosh.

Before we got a spin drier
The clothes through a mangle were pushed,
To squeeze out the extra water
It was a job that couldn't be rushed.

Then all the soggy, wet washing
Into a basket, thrown any old way,
And everyone was hoping and praying
That it was a good drying day.

The clothes were hung in the garden,
Having wiped over the washing line,
Secured by wooden dolly pegs,
Looking clean in the bright sunshine.

The line was hoisted upwards
By a long prop made of wood,
So the wind could surround them
Really drying the washing, as it should.

However if it WAS wet and rainy,
The clothes were hung on a wire,
Or placed over the wooden maiden
Which was set up by the fire.

The ironing was made easier
When we had something new,
An electric iron - all the rage,
Making the job quicker to do.

My Nan had a flat iron,
She had to heat on some coal,
But when she saw the new one
To buy it was her goal.

So washday was finally over,
At least Mum had finished, then
She had the rest of the house to clean
Until Monday came round again.

WASHDAY BLUES

Sharing this poem with your relative:

This poem recalls a time years ago before common usage of washing machines, spin or tumble driers. Washday was always on a Monday and without labour saving devices was very hard work. Washing clothes by hand and then trying to get them dry, particularly in the winter, could be a real struggle. People who had to use a mangle to wring out their clothes never forgot it; you had to be really strong. Without driers, fine weather was wished for, otherwise clothes had to be draped over wooden maidens or clothes horses or hung on racks that could be hoisted up to the ceiling.

Reminiscence Avenues

When discussing this poem it will be useful to have some vocabulary to use. The words and phrases will mean different things to different people. Here are some suggestions:

Pick 'N' Mix

Washtub, tongs, mangle, washing powder, bags
of starch

Shirts, blankets, sheets, dolly pegs, washboard

Pounding, rinsing, drying, steaming, cleaning

Tiring, exhausting, enjoying, satisfying

Clean, sparkling, whiter than white, stained,
heavy

Damp, overwhelming, busy, time-consuming,
important

Top Tip: Washday was often a job where
neighbours helped each other. Ask a friend who
remembers 'Washday Blues' to come in for a
chat with you and your relative. There will be
plenty of stories!

Personal Reminiscences:

'You could make little dolls with those pegs. I
used to love making the clothes and drawing in
the faces.'

'The mangle was such hard work – so difficult to turn…'

'I remember one washing powder gave away plastic roses with each box to get you to buy more…'

Celebrations

We're celebrating a birthday
A very special day
I'm buying a card and present
To send without delay.
So making a cake is a must
With icing and jam inside,
And on the top some candles
I can't wait for it to be tried.

We're enjoying a wedding
A very special day
I'm buying a card and present
To send without delay.
I'm looking forward to seeing
The bride dressed up in white
The groom, scared, but excited,
And dancing through the night.

We're remembering an anniversary

A very special day,

I'm buying a card and present

To send without delay.

I've got the date in my diary

From years long ago,

It's so special to celebrate

With all those who you know.

We're please to announce a birth

A very special day

I'm buying a card and present

To send without delay.

Matinee jackets for new borns,

Bootees and bonnet too.

I can't wait to see the child

And if it's pink or if it's blue.

Congratulations you've got a degree
A very special day
I'm buying a card and present
To send without delay.
You've worked extremely hard
For almost three long years
Now you're in your cap and gown
We raise you lots of cheers.

We love those special occasions
That make a special day
When we buy cards and presents
To send without delay.
It's great to share celebrations
With all those who you love
And joy and happiness abound
With rainbows from above.

CELEBRATIONS

Sharing this poem with your relative:

There were plenty of occasions to celebrate in post-war Britain; even though such events were often not as elaborate as today. Parties were often held at home or in village halls. In houses, doors were sometimes taken off to make more space available. As well as greetings cards, people would also send special messages of congratulations in telegrams delivered by GPO boys. They were called 'The Red Bike Boys.' These young boys liked delivering to weddings as they were often given a sixpence, (a tanner) for a photograph with the bride.

Reminiscence Avenues

Your relative may have good recall of special celebrations in their life. Many older people can remember their first day at school, wedding day, or birth of a child. This poem celebrates such occasions and the happiness of 'buying a card and present' for many special events. The repeating lines in each verse are an opportunity for your relative to join in with you as you read it. Here are some questions to help evoke memories.

Questions

Can you remember a favourite birthday present?

Did you receive money gifts in your birthday cards?

What birthday cakes can you remember making for you or your children / grandchildren?

Where did you get married?

Do you remember the bouquet / buttonhole you wore for your wedding?

What are the following anniversaries known as – 25th, 30th, 40th, 50th, 60th? (Silver, Pearl, Ruby, Golden, Diamond)

What did you do to celebrate your anniversaries?

What preparations did you make for a new baby in the family?

Can you remember how you felt with a new baby

in the family?

Did you or a member of your family graduate?

Did you make any cards or presents to give on special occasions?

Top Tip: This poem can be enhanced by a collection of birthday cards, graduation photos or a wedding album.

Personal Reminiscences:

'We celebrated our 60th wedding anniversary and got a special card from The Queen… Lovely. We wrote to say thank you.'

'We had congratulation telegrams for our wedding delivered by the GPO boy.'

'I'm 95 – do you like my birthday badge? It's great to celebrate.'

Albert's pet shop

There's a little old shop called Albert's
That's right at the end of our street,
It's where Mum and Dad would take me
When they wanted to give me a treat.

Now Albert's was a pet shop
He sold all kind of things
From rabbits, hamsters and gerbils,
To budgies with blue wings.

It smelled of old wet sawdust,
It smelled of many thick furs,
The bubble of tanks of exotic fish,
And the noise of woofs and purrs.

We gawped in through the window
All the animals we could see
But my very favourite-est one
Was a Jack Russell puppy.

At last after much persuasion
My family finally gave way
And for little pup, things looked up,
As she came home with me one day.

Our household was never tidy
From that day on 'til now
Always white hairs on the carpet
And a constant bow wow wow.

But I loved my little puppy,
Bonnie B was her name
I trained her in the garden,
And she loved to play a game.

We went everywhere together
The two of us, a muddle
But my mother got kind of cross
When on the floor appeared a puddle…

My Uncle Joe liked animals,
And he went to Albert's place
Chose himself two rabbits
My Aunt said he was in disgrace.

But Uncle looked after the rabbits
And built them a wooden hutch
He called them Fred and Tommy
And loved them very much.

But just a few months later
In time, before you knew,
Joe found quite shockingly,
In the hutch there were more than two.

On further investigation
Joe found he was quite right,
Seems Fred was really Freda,
Some babes had been born at night.

Animals are good companions
Our neighbour, Mrs Lane, had heard
And looking around Albert's emporium
After considering, chose a bird.

She bought a large cage for the creature
And millet, a swing and a mirror so
The budgie would be occupied
With this she named him Joe.

Joey was bluish all over
He liked to play on his swing
He preened himself in his mirror
But never once did he sing.

My friend Annie bought a goldfish,
That lived in a big glass bowl,
She then bought two more
Was she saving for a shoal?

Albert's shop has given pleasure

With animals great and small,

The world is better with Albert's

And I have my beautiful Bonnie Ball.

ALBERT'S PET SHOP

Sharing this poem with your relative:

Years ago it was commonplace to have pet shops
with many animals for sale in high streets. Today
this can be controversial; but for our purposes
this is a light-hearted poem that your relative will
enjoy. Many people owned a variety of pets and
they were usually bought at a pet shop. When
you visited a pet shop years ago you were often
deafened by the sounds of puppies barking,
parrots squawking and cats miaowing.

Reminiscence Avenues

This poem highlights the pleasures and pitfalls of
pet ownership. You can help bring this poem to
life by preparing a collection of photos and
pictures.

This is a longer poem to include different animals
and can be read all at once or in parts to suit your
relative.

Photo Album

Create your own album by using photos of family pets. Talk about their names, their favourite foods, their funny little ways, (or not so funny) and what animal was their favourite.

If your relative did not own pets, but likes animals, collect pictures from magazines or the Internet of a variety of domestic animals.

Top Tip: Your relative may like a visit from a neighbour's pet if they do not have one of his or her own. A lovable and placid pooch that loves to be stroked can be very beneficial for everyone. (Please do your own risk assessment.)

Personal Reminiscences:

'I was sent out to get some nails for the shed but passing the pet shop I saw this tiny ball of fluff in the window. It was a puppy – and it came home with me – and the nails.'

'I always remember the smell in a pet shop –
straw, sawdust, fur and… worse!'

'We had a tortoise – it stayed in the garden…'

Shopping

Think about your High Street, fifty years ago.
Where are those much-loved shops that we used
to know?

I'd pop into the family baker's when I went to
town with Mum
For two fresh white loaves and a sticky currant
bun.
The shop was full of bread and always smelled a
treat
We'd carefully choose some cream cakes –
delicious to eat.

The grocer's was halfway down another certain
street
Off a block they cut your cheese that reeked of
smelly feet.
Our biscuits were bought from a box, and
weighed by the pound,

In tins, fruit and ham and spam could usually be found.

At the butcher's we bought our meat, Dewhurst was the best,
They laid out chicken portions, a cut above the rest.
Our bacon was sliced thinly, by the cutting machine
And Mum would ask for a Sunday joint – and 'to make it lean'.

The market was a busy place, with people shouting wares,
'Red ripe apples, purple grapes, bananas and juicy pears.'
There was a man selling tripe, another flogging fish,
An ironmonger with as many shovels as you wish.

To buy our shoes we had a choice from Dolcis or from Clarks,
Or Freeman Hardy and Willis, just up from Marks.
This is where we bought our clothes, with the St Michael label,
Furniture from the Co-op – chairs and a Formica table.

When I had thruppence, I could go to the sweetie shop
Where in jars were gobstoppers and sour Acid drops
Sherbet fountains, Spangles, Mars and Milky Way…
We were hurried along, as deciding took all day.

In Woolworth's we could stand and bag a Pic 'N' Mix
While Mum chose a colour for her new lipsticks,

Then onto the newsagents for a Beano comic read

And Mum would buy a newspaper and the

stamps she'd need.

The chemist we visited was Boots or Timothy

White's,

There we'd get our medicine, they knew what

was right.

And then a rest, a cup of tea at Lyons or the

Kardomah

Or a meaty Wimpy snack in my favourite coffee

bar.

Thinking about my High Street, fifty years ago.

Where are those much-loved shops that we used

to know?

SHOPPING

Sharing this poem with your relative:
This poem highlights those shops that were commonplace in post-war Britain. During those times high streets had many small independent shops and were full of character. The chain stores also tended to be smaller than those of today; this meant high streets in towns and cities were very different to one another.

Reminiscence Avenues
Your relative will enjoy this walk down a high street bustling with variety. They may remember shopping in other shops too. Below are some questions to stimulate recollections.

Verse by Verse
Verse 1 Ask your relative to reflect on their High Street years ago.
Verse 2 What is your favourite cake?
Verse 3 What was a cheap way to buy biscuits

then? (Broken biscuits were put in a tin and sold off cheaply.)

Verse 4 What is meant by 'to make it lean'?

Verse 5 What other stalls can you remember in the market place years ago?

Verse 6 What size shoe do you take?

Verse 7 What were / are Flying Saucers, Black Jacks, Fruit Salads, Spangles, Refreshers, Love Hearts, Sweet cigarettes, Allsorts?

Verse 8 How did they serve the ketchup in the Wimpy bar? (In a bright red plastic tomato.)

Verse 9 What other shops can your relative remember?

Top Tip: Take a few photos yourself of independent high street shops today like the butcher's, greengrocer's and baker's. Share these with your relative to evoke memories.

Personal Reminiscences:

'I loved getting the 83 bus to Wembley High Road to go shopping. We always went on the top deck. When we got to C and A the conductor shouted, 'C and A – get your uniforms here!'

'We always bought fresh made bread from Higgins the Bakers. They got up early to make fresh bread every day. The smell was wonderful.'

'We looked forward to spending our pocket money on 1d (one penny) sweets – Black Jacks, Fruit Salads, Flying Saucers, Gobstoppers – such choice! The shopkeeper got tired of the children filling the shop and taking their time to choose…'

On his hobby horse

My Dad's had many hobbies
Too many for you to guess,
But I'll tell you some of them
You're sure to be impressed.

Once he took up DIY
With a workshop in his shed,
But gave up after the shelf he'd made
Fell down upon his head.

So taking on a sporting challenge,
He ran and jogged round town
But tired and hot and sweaty
It soon got the thumbs down.

A more sedentary occupation
Was following a football team
To see them in the final
Had always been a dream.

But the team all had two left feet
And at season end were relegated
He packed away his scarf and rattle
And the woeful team he slated.

Moving on to cricket season,
Dressed up all in white
He bowled a maiden over
But when batting got a fright.

The ball it came towards him
As hard and fast as can be
Howzat! LBW was the call -
He was walking back for tea.

So fishing seemed more gentle
A simple solitary sport,
The only trouble was
Not a fish nor eel was caught.

Then someone suggested
A fascinating game
To stand on a railway platform
And to note down every train.

He only tried this once
For a bit of a lark
But the trains all seemed to be the same
Just diesels in the dark.

Looking for something new to do
He did not need go far
It was there shining on the drive
His beloved Ford Anglia car.

He spent the weekend washing
Waxing and polishing too,
But looking under the bonnet
It was clear he didn't have a clue.

So other things he took up
To stimulate his brain
Included stamp collecting
And piloting a plane.

He wasn't into reading,
Coin collecting left him cold
Model making was a disaster
Swimming had no hold.

So searching for something different
Another thing to do
He took us all out walking
And before you knew...

We loved Dad's latest hobby
Outdoors in the great fresh air
Hiking, wandering all over
A hobby for us to share!

ON HIS HOBBY HORSE

Sharing this poem with your relative:
Your relative may have fond memories of hobbies they have tried in the past. Some may have been short lived, others become a lifelong passion. This poem includes a wide variety of post-war hobbies with men in mind, but can also be enjoyed by women. Memories of football matches with noisy rattles and fishing trips, which often ended with empty nets, evoke a time of simple pleasures. If reading this poem with female relatives, they may have enjoyed similar hobbies and also knitting, embroidery, hockey or reading. It is likely that your relative may have hobbies to tell you about which you were not aware of and were quite unusual, for example designing gardens using shells.

Reminiscence Avenues
The questions below maybe useful prompts to help your relative remember their hobbies.

Questions

Can you remember a DIY project that went wrong or perhaps it actually worked?

Were you sporty in anyway, did you belong to a sports club?

What football team did you support? What division were they in?

Have you any memories of Cup Finals at Wembley or the World Cup in 1966?

Did you watch or play cricket? Did you prefer batting or bowling?

Did you prefer sea or coarse fishing? What was the biggest fish you ever caught or did it get away?

What cars did you own in the post war period? Was it an Anglia, Hillman Minx, A35 or something else?

Were you a collector of anything? (Cigarette cards, tea cards, stamps, postcards, coins etc.)

Did you enjoy your hobbies on your own or did the whole family join in?

Were you known in your community for your

hobby? For example, cake craft, knitting, upholstery, woodwork, sewing etc.

Top Tip: If you have a photograph or cine film of your relative enjoying hobbies in the past this can often evoke happy memories and start conversations.

Personal Reminiscences:
'When I went fishing I left my catch in the bath. I only remembered the next morning when my daughter screamed!'

'My hobby was knitting and crocheting. I made a lot of blankets whilst watching television.'

'I collected stamps and put them in albums with tiny hinges made of paper on the back.'

Shades of Autumn

Golden trees, orange and red,

Hedgehogs scurry over a damp leaf bed.

Ripe brown conkers all a-shine,

Hips in hedges, blackberries entwine.

Dew on the grass, birds on the wing

Cobwebs tie plants with fine white string.

In autumn this is my view,

Now tell me - how about you?

Cold chill of winter hints in the air,

Ripening of apple and golden pear.

Moisty mushrooms in earthy bed,

The mud on boots after walker's tread.

The wheat in the field when it's cut,

Plums and damsons, a purply glut.

In autumn these are fragrances I knew

Now tell me - how about you?

Call of the birds as they prepare to go south,
The flow of the stream to river mouth.
The plop and drop of sun ready fruit,
In the woods an owl's lonely hoot.
The crack and crackle of a warm bonfire,
The bell of a church and a harvest choir.
In autumn these haunting sounds issue,
Now tell me - how about you?

Apple pies and warming crumbles,
Plum puddings to stop tummy rumbles.
Fresh vegetables from gardens, podded peas
Runner beans, turnips all to please.
Jams and marmalades, sticky for soft bread
Harvest bounty means we're well fed.
In autumn these things I love to chew
Now tell me - how about you?

Kicking leaves and creating woodpiles

Stacking firewood for bonfire night smiles.

Fireworks bright in dark night sky

Shooting stars, soaring up high.

Making fairy furniture from acorns small

Closing the curtains 'gainst the early nightfall.

In autumn these things I love to do

Now tell me - how about you?

SHADES OF AUTUMN

Sharing the poem with your relative:

Autumn is a season of great beauty. Years ago
Harvest Festivals were celebrated in schools,
village halls and churches. 'We Plough the Fields
and Scatter' was a very popular hymn. The
produce on display was distributed afterwards to
the needy in the community. Some places held a
Harvest Supper for local people.

At this time of year, many children also made
'guys', (Guy Fawkes) to burn on the bonfire.
Before this they were perched on old prams or
go-carts and wheeled onto street corners. 'A
penny for the guy' was a cry heard throughout
towns and cities.

Reminiscence Avenues

Different seasons can evoke a variety of
memories. If you choose to read this poem with
your relative during the autumn it may well have
more impact. After you read the poem once,

perhaps read it again, but stop after every verse and talk about the contents.

Verse by verse

What colours did the trees turn in autumn?
How did you play conkers; what did you do to make the conkers 'stronger'?
How did you play 'bobbing for apples'?
What fruits can you pick in autumn?
What memories do you have of Harvest Festivals at school or in church?
What does 'gathering the harvest' mean to you?
What was your favourite hot pudding? Were you allowed 'seconds'?
How did you make jam / chutney / pickles?
What memories have you got of Bonfire Nights?
What does 'A penny for the guy' mean?

Top Tip: Collect leaves and conkers with your relative if you can or bring them indoors to show. Step on a few leaves to hear them crunch and crackle to evoke memories.

Personal Reminiscences:

'I remember the bonfire smell, smoky and when you got near it was really hot...'

'I remember the school stage creaking with the weight of fruit and vegetables for the Harvest Festival. The colours were beautiful and the smell was... so fragrant!'

'I like the colours of the trees in Autumn... reds, yellows... a beautiful time of year.'

ACKNOWLEDGEMENTS

We would like to thank all the care and nursing homes we have worked in, for listening to our poetry and giving us such positive feedback. We have so enjoyed being part of your community during our activities and have loved listening to the reminiscences of the residents, relatives and staff.

We have found that listening to memories, especially those triggered by our poems, enhances our knowledge of someone. We have followed them down their Reminiscence Avenues to learn the smaller details of their earlier lives.

We would also like to thank our families and friends who have listened and given their thoughts on our poems - we loved hearing your recollections.

Finally we would like to thank you for buying this book. We hope you will have happy hours sharing our poems with your relative, friend or patient. We would love to hear your stories at info@bonnie-day.co.uk

Printed in Great Britain
by Amazon